LEONORIAN WITCHCRAFT

Also by Leonora Jackson

Powerful Magic – Secrets from the Inner Circle
A Handbook for Metaphysics.

LEONORIAN WITCHCRAFT

A New Religion

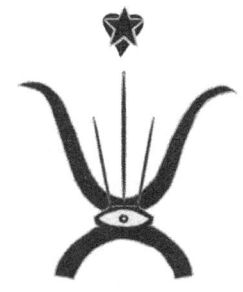

And General Workbook for Adepts

Leonora Jackson

LEONORIAN WITCHCRAFT
A New Religion
and General Workbook for Adepts

Published by * Leonora * in Australia 2017
First published, in part, online by Leonora Jackson 1997

Copyright © 1997 to present Leonora Jackson

The Author asserts the moral right to
be identified as the author of this work.

ISBN-13 (TPB) colour:: 978-0-9803560-4-5
ISBN-13 (TPB): 978-0-9803560-5-2
ISBN-13 (USLPB) colour:: 978-0-9803560-6-9

ISBN-13 (Special Edition HC): 978-0-9803560-7-6

Cover Art © 2017 Leonora Jackson

Coven Insignia created by Leonora Jackson.

All rights reserved.
No part of this publication may be used or
reproduced in any manner, stored in a retrieval system,
or transmitted in any form or by any means, electronic, mechanical,
photocopying, recording or otherwise, without the prior
written permission of the author.

The Circle Signs Layout is a **registered trade mark**.
You may display the Circle Signs Layout on your
altar mirror for personal use only.

For more information please read
"Powerful Magic – Secrets from the Inner Circle"
A Handbook for Metaphysics.

leonorianwitchcraft.com

Table of Contents

A LITTLE CLEARING..XII
SELF EXPRESSION - A LITTLE HISTORY...XVI
    TAKE HEED...21
DECLARATION & EXPLANATION...25
    What is Leonorian Witchcraft?..28
    On Worship and Creating Deities..32

for NEOPHYTES..35
    The Crown of Strength Heart and Wisdom explained..........................38
    The "Cupped Hands" Closing..40
    I am Here..43
OPENING THE CIRCLE..47
    Circle Opening and Raising the Energy of the Signs............................48
A DAILY RITUAL...51
    A DAILY RITUAL WITH THE CYCLE of CREATION.........................52

for INITIATES..55
    DOCTRINE and DOGMA..58
    21 DAY PREPARATION FOR INITIATION..62
MIRROR WORKINGS...65
    MIRROR RITUAL...66
    MIRROR RITUAL 1...68
FOUR POINTS OF THE PYRAMID..71
    A Calling and Drawing In Ritual for Daily Use.....................................76
    Sit Like a Witch...78
    I am Here..80

for ACOLYTES...83
    A Calling and Drawing In Ritual..86
    Circle Opening and Raising the Energy of the Signs............................89
    ADDENDUM...94

for INNER CIRCLE ADEPTS...97
    A Hex Chant and Banishing Ritual...101
    Death and Passing Over Utterance...102
    Release and Excommunication Ritual..104
TRANSFORM..107
    Circle Opening and Raising the Energy of the Signs..........................108
    I am Here..110
    Flow Between Worlds..112
THE GRAND CEREMONY...117
    The Path of the Grand Ceremony...118
    The Grand Ceremony...120

The Three Great Circles of Magic..124

about Leonora

Leonora Teaches and Practises a form of Witchcraft based on
lessons learned during 22 years of training with Grand
Master Edgar Pielke within the Australian branch
of the Great White Brotherhood of Light.

Extended and enriched, this form is now called
"Leonorian Witchcraft", a title first bestowed upon
it by certain, rather keen coven members, and
finally accepted and approved by Leonora.

Leonora currently lives in Sydney, Australia
with a much-loved companion and many candles.

1 + 1

=

A Little Clearing

Warm greetings everyone.

Edgar Pielke (Eddie) was my Mentor, a Druid Master and "The Old Sorcerer" as he liked to call himself, but he didn't write
the Doctrine and Dogma of our Practice.

He taught it.

The Doctrine and Dogma form part of very old 'mouth to ear' Teachings from the Inner Circle of the Hermetic Order of the Great White Brotherhood of Light - one of those ancient mystery schools.

Eddie first learned some of it from his father and step-mother, who were members of a Coven in Germany.

He then learned more from another Brotherhood member who, as I recall Eddie telling me, was 'Julius Fischer', an Austrian professor he met under extreme conditions in a concentration camp, and who recognised Eddie as a young Practitioner, offering him support and further information, including the hidden and secret Knowledge of the Signs and the Cycle of Creation.

Armed with this valuable and hard-won Wisdom, Eddie brought what he had learned to Australia, where he founded the Australian branch of the Brotherhood.

He was my Mentor for 22 years.

After Eddie stepped back from Teaching in 1992, and based on what I had learned from him, I put together the overview that forms the Diagram of the Three Great Circles of Magic.

In 1997, during a Mirror Ritual, I was deeply 'called' to offer that information to the public, along with some guidelines describing the flow of the Cycle of Creation.
So I published it, in part, to my website.

Ten years later, after listening to Guidance, much contemplation, and further research, I published "Powerful Magic - Secrets from the Inner Circle", an extremely useful handbook for Seekers who wish to study the flow of the Cycle, the Three Great Circles of Magic, and learn more about the history of the Brotherhood in Australia and my involvement in it.

It's mandatory reading for those who wish
to Practise this form of the Craft.

Since then I've gathered together all the Doctrine and Dogma that
formed the basis of the ancient Teachings of the Brotherhood,
usually only offered "Mouth to Ear" as needed over time.

Now, our Sacred and long-hidden Lore is in one
place and easily accessible for you to find.

I have also experienced the joys, pleasures, and challenges of creating
carefully crafted inclusions to the Lore that not only enrich the
Teachings, but will, I hope, inspire all dedicated Seekers,
Students, Practitioners and Teachers to expand
their Understanding of the Craft.

This is why I've made the distinction between the Teachings
of the Brotherhood as I learned them and the new,
augmented Form you will find within these pages:
So that the new information nurtured within the Great Circle of the
Order of the Red Rose, which is standing on the shoulders of
Giants, is understood to enliven and inspire the Teachings of the
Brotherhood, while growing and prospering as its enriched Inner Circle.

I wrote the Declaration in order to define our new Rituals and
Workings as blossomed Inner Circle Guidance, and to mark a
clear delineation in Time between the Old and New forms.

The newly created Insignia, Rituals, Information, and Workings,
in naturally flowing combination with the Old Teachings, are
now being offered through the Great and Inner Circles
of the Order of the Red Rose as the Inner Circle
Metaphysics of Leonorian Witchcraft.

To Clear the Path and Open Doors that have been closed too long.

May your days and nights be Blessed.
In the Service of the Craft.

Ipsissima xx
Leonora

0

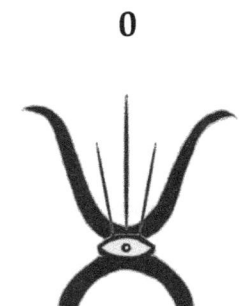

Self Expression - a little history

I can't tell you how hard it was for me to accept that
this Working had achieved a "beautiful" result.

Believe it or not, for much of my life I've felt as though there
was nothing I could do that was "beautiful" – ever.

I thought everything I did was either 'not good enough'
(my opinion) or 'up yourself' (the opinion of others).

There are lots of reason why I might have started thinking like that,
but the one thing from the dim, dark past that comes to mind is
that it seemed to me every time I achieved something with any
kind of ease, my young contemporaries started saying I was
'up myself' or 'too good', although I had no idea what that meant.

I have to admit that, when it happened, being good at
something gave me real pleasure, but it wasn't because
I thought I was "Too Good" for anyone else.
I'd never even considered that.

Home and school life at the time had given me the impression that
learning quickly and efficiently was the thing to do, and, in the
areas where I was able to succeed, I simply loved doing it.
I also loved the way it made my parents and teachers happy, and
I couldn't understand why anyone wouldn't enjoy the whole process.

However, "up myself", whatever that was, was something I
learned I didn't want to be, because it caused most of my
school friends to dislike me, and made me an outcast.
Because I was 'different'.

So, after a while I not only tried to not be up myself, I
intentionally tried not to be good at very much at all.

This included, but was not limited to use of language, musical
ability, general understanding of 'how things worked', and
my innate ability to learn quickly – as though I could
'intuit' what our teachers were showing us.

I started being bad at stuff I knew I could be
good at, in case I upset my school friends.

Then I got migraines. Bad ones.
I started wagging school.
You know what I mean.

Not that I was particularly bright in the general scheme of things either,
but by then I had dumbed myself down so much that, eventually, I
was afraid to do anything insightful in case I did something
'too clever' and accidentally offended someone.

To that end, I gave away many things I could never get back.
Including, no doubt, whatever self-esteem I had left, and my sanity.
Because I was led to believe it was for the best.

The backlash of all that "help" slowly drove me to being overly
assertive as a defensive measure on one hand, and on
the other to a crippling sense of self-pity that
was, at times, almost insurmountable.

Psychiatry didn't help.
Neither did Religion.
And don't get me started on Psychoanalysis.

Apparently no-one could usefully help me with any of this, or answer any
of my still burning questions about 'life, the universe, and everything'.

I swear, if it hadn't been for learning about the Cycle of Creation, the Law of
the Paradox, and the Doctrinal guidance I received from Eddie (Edgar
Pielke) during my time as a Student in the Great White Brotherhood
of Light, I probably would have done myself in a long time ago.

The information I learned from him clarified almost everything
for me, and I am eternally grateful that I was lucky enough,
curious enough, and 'up myself' enough to understand it.
And, for his Patience.

In a strange twist of fate, if I hadn't been living rough
in King's Cross at the time I might never have met him.

I'm not, by any means, suggesting that studying this or any part of the
Craft, or any religion or philosophy for that matter, will help anyone
overcome suicidal tendencies, or anything else that troubles them.

It did for me because this old Mouth-to-Ear style of Witchcraft "Mysteries" offered me information I was hungry to learn.
That is, I was so interested in learning the information that I had to put my insecurities to one side in order to be clear-headed enough to take it all in, and then to learn how to make it work.

It also gave me the tools to help me put those insecurities to one side, and to deal with them if and when they arose.
But, again, that wasn't my main focus.

Long story short, I wasn't driven by a need to overcome anything.
Or to "find myself".

I was driven by a hunger to understand certain things.

I had questions that religion, philosophy, and even other Forms of Witchcraft didn't, wouldn't, or couldn't answer.
I wanted useful, logical, magical(!) Answers. And there they were.

Anyway, before anyone decides that I'm sharing some of the more fragile areas of my personal history (something I rarely do) so that I can promote this book, let me say:
That's exactly what I'm doing.

The reason I wrote this book and consequently, inadvertently, created a whole, New Form of Witchcraft is because some Red Rose coven members asked if the Brotherhood had any Rituals or Ceremonies, and I had to say it didn't.

So, I wrote some. For them.

Not because I'm 'up myself' (although, by now I probably am), but to give my Coven members a deeper experience
of the flow of our Form of the Craft.
One that was less "Mouth-to-Ear" and more "Immersive".

It wasn't until I'd written our new Rituals, Meditations, Workings and Ceremonies – testing them, re-writing them, seeing if they worked for our members etc. - that I finally stood back and looked at the overall result, as a painter finally steps back to get the full view of their work after being so close to the canvas for so long.

Well, I just cried. I could hardly believe it!

It was awe-inspiring, and it took everything I had
within me to not feel inordinately pleased, joyful – ecstatic
really – and, yes, Eddie, I admit it, PROUD of my own work.
(See the Doctrine & Dogma for context).

Apparently, the coven members who inspired
me to create it felt the same way.

It's their love, encouragement, (eagle-eyed proof reading) and 'Wow Lees'
that kept me going when I wasn't sure if I was on the right track.
You know who you are, and I can't thank you enough.

I'm still nervous about calling it 'beautiful' - even though it
clearly is - because I'm still harbouring my little secret.
Of not wanting to appear up myself.

I need to say, if it comes across that way, it's not my intention,
nor is it in any way the reason I put my heart and soul
into the development of this new Form.

I did it because, once I'd started, I was driven
by an overwhelming need to continue.
To give my Coven members something enriching
and wonderful to work with.

And I simply couldn't stop until I had achieved that to the best of my ability.

With this in mind, I now offer this 'beautiful' and extraordinarily moving
(for me) creation to you, in the hope that you will enjoy it, find some
new strings for your Magical bow, and gain a deep, experiential
Understanding of these beautiful Inner Circle Mysteries.

In Strength Heart and Wisdom.

Thank you.

Leonora
Ipsissima xxi

SEEKER

TAKE HEED

*Of this gentle request.
For the Wise to follow.
And the Fool to reject.*

*It's all here
in Order, for your weal or woe.
So, follow the Path
at the Level you Know.
In your true Stand of
Knowledge.
And Flow.*

INHALE

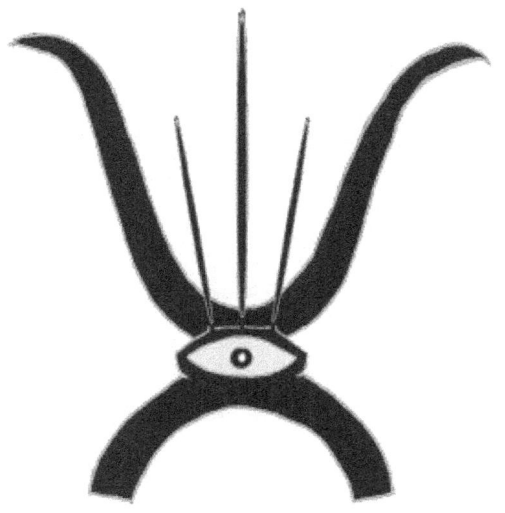

Strength Heart and Wisdom

1
DECLARATION & EXPLANATION

THE GREAT CIRCLE
of THE ORDER of THE RED ROSE

As Above - So Below

Inner Circle Declaration of Continuity

Founded by Leonora on the 14th of June 2000, The Great Circle of the Order of the Red Rose carries the Flame and Inner Circle Knowledge taught to her by Grand Master Edgar Pielke during her 22 years of Study within the Australian branch of The Hermetic Order of the Great White Brotherhood of Light, a Universal tradition that contained and taught the Inner Circle Mysteries of Creationist Magic.

Nurtured by and raised within the heart of the Inner Circle of the Australian branch of The Hermetic Order of The Great White Brotherhood of Light, and Inspired by the Knowledge of Creationist Magic gained therein, the Great Circle of the Order of the Red Rose now Claims as its Outer Court and its Inner Circle.

A Universal tradition that aims to offer Mind Over Matter techniques designed to affect Change, and to increase the availability of Inner Circle information as taught within the Australian branch of the Brotherhood, The Great Circle of the Order of the Red Rose is now even more enriched with newly created Insignia, Ceremonies, Rituals, and Information.

The main Aim of the Red Rose Circle is to guide Seekers in a way that best suits them and the Study.
Ultimately, as well as a doorway into the Mysteries of Creation, the Circle seeks to create an environment that allows for balance between personal freedom and Spiritual understanding.

A Seeker may remain a member of the Outer Court of the Great Circle of the Order of the Red Rose for as long as they desire with no requirement to advance further. Membership here requires only the desire to be known as a member, and to bring to its highest potential the idea that this is A Circle of Magic and Mystery - of Love and Balance.

THE GREAT CIRCLE
of THE ORDER of THE RED ROSE

As Above - So Below

Inner Circle Declaration of Continuity

As with the Australian branch of the Great White Brotherhood of Light, the Great and Inner Circles of the Order of the Red Rose contain and teach the Mysteries of Creationist Magic now called Leonorian Witchcraft. Access from the Outer Court through the Portal to Guidance is by Initiation only.

Initiated Membership to the Great Circle of the Order of the Red Rose may be offered by Leonora or her authorised representative(s), or it may be requested by the Seeker.
Applicants will be either approved or rejected based on their individual understanding of publicly available Outer Court information.

This group is not affiliated with any Rosicrucian orders, and does NOT include "Aureae Crucis" (Cross of Gold) in its title.

The Great Circle of the Order of the Red Rose is
A Circle of Magic and Mystery
Of Love and Balance.
Members around the world are called by the desire to
bring this Understanding to its Highest Potential.

With Love

In the Service of the Craft.

Leonora Jackson
Inner Circle Maga/Ipsissima of
The Great Circle of the Order of the Red Rose.

Dated: 20th March 2017
Sydney, Australia

THE GREAT CIRCLE
of THE ORDER of THE RED ROSE

Strength Heart and Wisdom

What is Leonorian Witchcraft?

We are not "All One"
We are not the same.

We each have our own approach to the Mysteries.
We each imbue ourselves with what works
for us based on the Teachings.

Each changeable opinion bringing
a new depth to the Study.

We do not follow the Rule of Three.
We understand Nature loves Balance and will
exact a price in order to achieve it.

We Know what that price is.

We Open our Circle at the beginning, not the end of our Rites.
We Close all Circles with a simple act of Thanks.

To call this form of Witchcraft by a specific name is not to
re-title that which already exists in other Forms.

It is unique.
It contains information not found in other Forms.

It is not Wicca, though it loves the Moon.
It is not Buddhism, though that is its closest neighbour.

THE GREAT CIRCLE
of THE ORDER of THE RED ROSE

Strength Heart and Wisdom

What is Leonorian Witchcraft?

It is Witchcraft.
It Teaches what hides behind the Veil of Worship.

It has specific Insignia, Rituals and Information
newly created for purpose by its Founder.

It has Doctrine and Dogma and Understandings
brought forward from Old Knowledge.

It a Universal tradition that Teaches the
Mysteries of Creationist Magic.

It offers this Wisdom using the Cycle
of Creation as a guide.

Its Covenstead is the Great Circle of
the Order of the Red Rose.

It is popularly named after its Founder
as Leonorian Witchcraft.

It is Inner Circle Metaphysics.

In the Service of the Craft.

Ipsissima xx
Leonora
16 April 2017

ON WORSHIP and CREATING DEITIES

On Worship and Creating Deities

Inner Circle Metaphysics and Leonorian Witchcraft define the Craft as a series of mysterious but discoverable actions, events, and information designed to create specific conditions that can Open the Way to an increasingly deeper and more direct interaction with the Known and the Unknown aspects of whatever the Practitioner considers to be the Divine within Nature.

Worshipping a personified aspect of Nature is often the first and only step some people ever take along that Path.

The Craft techniques used in both Levels of the Outer Circle rely on Belief, Worship and Faith in Deities which are first Imagined, created, named, and personified by the Practitioners, then projected and made real so that they can be Worshipped and called upon for assistance.

Outer Circle Practitoners of the First Level, which includes all religious denominations that use Worship and Faith, are taught either deliberately or by omission to overlook or ignore this process, and sometimes even dispute when asked their active involvement in it at all, while at the same time being required to Worship without question the Personified result: representations of the preferred Gods or Goddesses – one or many.

Our Form of the Craft does not teach or use the Outer Circle methods of Worship and Faith.

Its Teachings are not based in any kind of fear-based or superstitious belief structure.

Its Doctrinal guidelines say: "You are god, you are the devil, yours is the choice", and it defines "Spirit" as 'That Which Animates', suggesting no need or requirement for worship within that definition.

On Worship and Creating Deities

It does not Teach or require its Practitioners to dedicate themselves to, believe in, follow, or worship any God, Goddess, Lord, or Lady.

In fact, and as a strict safety requirement for Neophytes, it directly cautions against those actions For Any Reason unless and until the Practitioner Understands and uses Paradox Law for the purpose.

When, and as long as the Law of the Paradox and the Knowledge of Projected Reality is functionally incorporated into their Practice, and Know Thyself is paramount, the Practitioner may, if they wish, immerse themselves in direct communication and interaction with Projected and Personified Entities – Deities and 'Spirits' of all and any kind - whether apprehended or invoked.

At Will.

Now no longer 'hopeful' worship, but a powerful Mind over Matter technique.

Second Level, Outer Circle Practitioners who choose to go beyond the need for Worship can start to see that there is more to the Craft than Faith alone, and perhaps even question what that might be and how it works.

Practitioners of the First Level of the Middle Circle and above are taught to acknowledge their role in the process, learn how it works, activate it, then deeply enjoy it for what it is:

A manifested, direct, Liminal and Magical interaction with the Known and the Unknown.

In the Service of the Craft.
Ipsissima xx

for NEOPHYTES

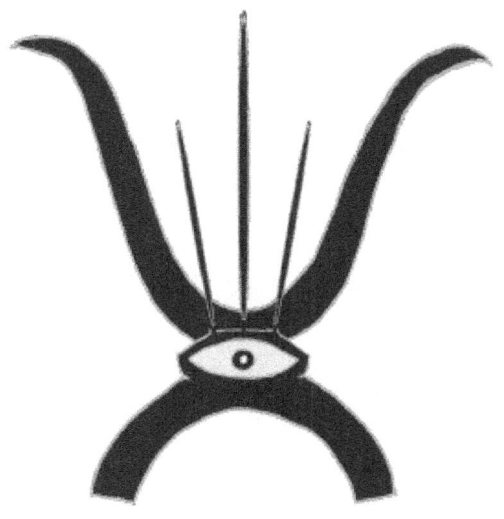

Strength Heart and Wisdom

2
BEGINNINGS

ABOUT OUR INSIGNIA

The Crown of Strength Heart and Wisdom explained.

For those who wish to delve Deeper into the Mysteries of the Great Circle of the Order of the Red Rose and Leonorian Witchcraft.

Please contemplate this deeply before commencing any version of our Ceremonial Rituals:

The Inner Circle Understanding that inspired me to create our beautiful Insignia by including Three glowing Candles within the Opened Horns of Fate, atop the Eye of Self Knowledge says:

Strength equals Tolerance
Heart equals Patience
Wisdom equals Understanding
and
The Crown of Strength, Heart, and Wisdom is also
The Chalice of Tolerance, Patience, and Understanding.

One, States of Being within our Order - the other, the Tools of our Craft.

You Draw one in, while at the same time immersing yourself in the other.

A Magical double action which is neither Irony nor Paradox, but just as amusingly poignant.

The simple act of observing our Insignia now sparks a Deep, Clear yet Occult Understanding.

ABOUT OUR INSIGNIA

The Crown of Strength Heart and Wisdom explained.

Feel it.

When you Draw In one, you Call In the other equally.
They are not the same, nor interchangeable. They do not
overlap, conflate, nor subsume.

However, they each contain their alternate attributes equally.

Consider this.
Allow this.
Agree to this at the same time that you agree with our
Knowledge of the Mirror's attributes.

Hover softly on that knife edge, leaning in both directions at Once.

And Let Go.

Then, commence the Circle Opening and
Raising the Energy of the Signs.

In the Service of the Craft.

Ipsissima xx
Leonora

The "Cupped Hands" Closing

To thank the Altar, the Ancient Covens in the Mirror, and to Close any of our Rituals.

A Ritual Closing for you from the Great
and Inner Circles of the Order of the Red Rose.

The "Cupped Hands" closing mentioned in the 'general' version
of the Circle Opening and Raising the Energy of the Signs
starts by putting the edges of your palms together to make a
cup shape, then moving the cup towards your chest
as though you were about to drink.

The action is done in one smooth movement over
one comfortable inhale/exhale cycle.

This is a lovely way to Close of any of our Rituals:

With your head up and looking at your Reflection in the
Mirror, or facing your Altar if you don't have or are not using
a Mirror at the time, make that cupped shape with your
hands and lift your palms towards your chest
as though about to drink.

The "Cupped Hands" Closing

Bend your head down slightly towards the cup and INHALE

Look up, and with elbows still slightly bent, move your cupped palms towards the Mirror as though offering the 'water' to your Reflection.

Now, with your palms still facing upwards, spread your hands shoulder-width apart and smile your Thanks towards your Mirror, your Altar, and the Old Ones who visit.

Then move the opened palms back towards your shoulders and down along your body to your sides with a lovely, long sighed EXHALE.

Bow slightly forwards, then take a step back away from the Altar.

The Deed is Done.
In the Service of the Craft.

I am Here

Strength Heart and Wisdom
A Sacred Agreement and Understanding of the Magical Condition

The warning stands!
Everything That Is, and Everything That Is Not.

Know Thyself prevails throughout the whole Working.
The Adepts version should not be attempted by anyone who
is not at least of the Second Level, Middle Circle.

Please discover and research the Three Great Circles of Magic for clarity.

The idea behind all versions of this Working is twofold:
To extend the Liminal in order to deeply enhance all Rituals
and Ceremonies, and to bring the Practitioner gently but firmly
into Experiencing the Law of the Paradox, with the Acolytes and
Adepts version providing full and complete immersion deeply
inside the concept - without actually drawing attention to it.

You'll just comfortably find yourself there, with the strength
of your immersion being relative to the Level of
your ability and Understanding.

I think you know what I mean, and I hope you love this
Working as much as you enjoy the other Rituals.

It gave me great joy to Create it.

Ipsissima xx
Leonora

I am Here

Strength Heart and Wisdom
A Sacred Agreement and Understanding of the Magical Condition

As Welcome

This version of the Working can be used as a welcome to bring
a group together, and as preparation for Ritual if solo.
It can also be used solo as a quick 'refresh' if you're in
a hurry, or need to quickly centre yourself.
In a group setting the Acolyte or Adept
leading the group asks the questions.

To be performed **before** Opening the Circle.

Stand facing the Altar/Mirror with hands by your side, palms forward. Observe the Insignia and remind yourself or the gathering of what it represents, then answer these questions slowly and with Certainty:

Inhale. Exhale.

I am Here

Strength Heart and Wisdom
A Sacred Agreement and Understanding of the Magical Condition

Teacher: "Who are you?"
Answer: "I am Here."

Teacher: "What are you?"
Answer: "I am Here."

Teacher: "When are you?"
Answer: "I am Here."

Teacher: "Where are you?"
Answer: "I am Here."

Teacher: "Why are you?"
Answer: "I am Here."

Teacher: "How are you?"
Reply: "I am Here"

Teacher: "Time and Place?"
Reply: "Nowhere, and Here."

Teacher tilts head forward: "We thank you."

If using the Working solo as a quick 'refresh'
or centering, give Cupped Hands Thanks here.

Otherwise, all remain standing with palms forward while the leader opens the Circle Round and Round – or you do if solo. Then all place hands in First position, Raise the Energy of the Signs, and continue with the chosen Ceremonies or Rituals.

OPENING THE CIRCLE

Circle Opening and Raising the Energy of the Signs

TO CREATE AND OPEN OUR SACRED SPACE
FOR GENERAL AND SPECIFIC WORKINGS

Performed as though Calling the Quarters but with
Inner Circle Understanding and Intent.

Light your candles, Create your Space and Invoke the
Circle Opening Ritual as follows:

Starting at the 'top' of the Circle and facing the Altar,
turn left and walk around the circumference three times,
speaking the following lines slowly enough
so that one line takes one revolution:

1st round: "I walk the Circle round and round"

2nd round: "I walk the Circle round and round"

3rd round: "I walk the Circle round and round, and Round"

Stand in First Position: legs shoulder-width apart, the fingers
of your right hand resting on the palm of your left, the
tips of your thumbs touching, making an open
circle in front of your lower belly.

Gaze at the Signs on your Mirror and Invoke the First Breath
by inhaling through the circle made with your thumbs
and raising your hands up in front of your body
to create the Inverted Pyramid position:
Arms spread to a V shape above your head, palms up.

Call the Energy of the Signs into the Circle.

Circle Opening and Raising the Energy of the Signs

Holding the Inverted Pyramid position throughout,
state out loud to each Sign in turn:

To The Horns of Fate:
"I call upon All Potential to bring Everything that Is,
and Everything that Is Not into the Circle."

To the Sign of Transmission:
"I call upon Transmission to bring Information into the Circle."

To the Eye of Self Knowledge:
"I call upon the Eye of Knowledge to bring Wisdom into the Circle."

To the Sign of Change:
"I call upon Change to bring Possibility into the Circle."

To the Spirit of Water:
"I call upon the Spirit of Water to bring Desire into the Circle."

To the Bridge of Life:
"I call upon the Bridge of Life to bring the Life Force into the Circle."

To the Centre of Power:
"I call upon The Key to bring the Mysterious Knowledge
of the Past, Present, and Future into the Circle."

Draw in the Energy of the Open Circle as
you lower your arms to your sides, palms forward.
At this point you may perform any of our
Rituals, Rites, or Mirror Meditations.

A Calling and Drawing in (ADEPTS version) includes space
within it for other Spell or Craft Work, as outlined in
the Addendum attached to that version.

Otherwise, other Spell or Craft Work is done at the
end of your chosen Ritual or Meditation.

Cupped Hands Thanks to the Mirror finishes the
Ritual and Closes the Circle automatically.

A DAILY RITUAL

A DAILY RITUAL WITH THE CYCLE of CREATION
"Powerful Magic – Secrets from the Inner Circle"

Either standing or sitting in front of your Mirror:
With your right hand resting on top of your left palm, thumbs touching so that a small circle is formed between your thumbs and fingers, as though holding a small sphere, and level with your lower belly.

In one fluid motion.

Inhale slowly, allow your thumbs to part, and raise your hands up past your belly, chest, neck, and face until fully extended over your head - as though Offering a beam of energy up towards the sky.

Then, while continuing the inhalation, spread your arms wide to form the Inverted Pyramid pose.

Hold the breath, then visualise The First Sign coming down from Above through your Offering to gently rest on the top of your head.

Exhale very gently and softly, and, lowering your arms outwards and down to your sides, draw the image of the Sign into yourself.

Let it drift down towards your feet, let it go.

Softly hold the breath and bring your hands back to the starting position, right fingers cupped over left with thumbs touching forming a circle in front of your genitals.

Repeat the ritual with the next Sign, softly and gently, but with Strength and Focus, all the way around the Cycle until you have completed the Seventh Sign.

A DAILY RITUAL WITH THE CYCLE of CREATION
"Powerful Magic – Secrets from the Inner Circle"

Return to the starting position.

Then, inhale, raise your arms in Offering as before, but this time visualise the whole Cycle drifting down from Above.

Drawn it into yourself as you very softly exhale
and lower your arms to your sides.

Let it drift downwards, filling your body and gently resting there.

Let your arms rest at your sides, palms forward, fingers
gently pointing down towards the ground.

Remain still for three gentle breaths.

Open your eyes.

This completes the ritual.

Shrug your shoulders and gently roll your head from side to side.

Quickly inhale and exhale in a deep, contented sigh,
give Cupped Hands thanks to the Old Ones,
and enjoy the rest of your day or night.

Lxx

for INITIATES

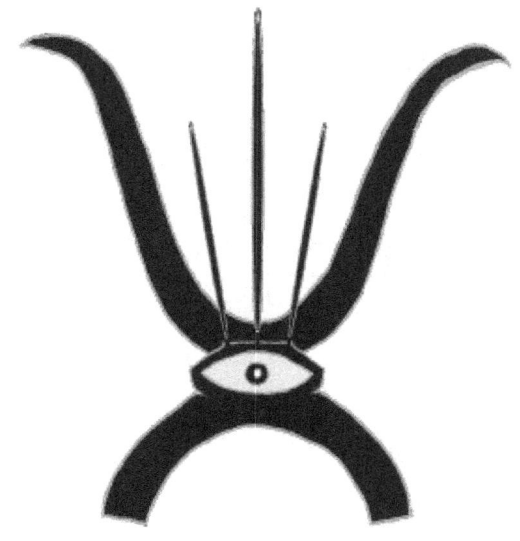

Strength Heart and Wisdom

3
DOCTRINE, DOGMA, PREPARATIONS & RITUALS

DOCTRINE and DOGMA
As taught within
THE GREAT CIRCLE OF THE ORDER OF THE RED ROSE

INNER CIRCLE GUIDELINES for LEONORIAN WITCHCRAFT
A Universal Tradition

Contemplating these points will trigger magical thinking.
Understanding and USING them will open the door.
And keep it open.

Nothing is for Nothing.
Nature and the Craft love Balance and always
exact a price in order to achieve it.
Be sure to pay it first, or it will be taken from you.
.

Now LET GO of all intolerance, self pity, and vanity.
.

Never hurt or harm anyone without a **justifiable** reason of Self Defence.
.

Forever control your emotions lest they control you.
Learn how to experience them deeply *and* turn
them on and off at will.
.

Forever live underneath your expectations so that your
ambitions do not drive you into discontent.
Let your success be a joy and a contentment - and not pride.
.

The 'Law of Three' says:
You in the centre, your Best on one side, your Worst on the other.

Working the Fulcrum is forever the Magic of it.
.

DOCTRINE and DOGMA
As taught within
THE GREAT CIRCLE OF THE ORDER OF THE RED ROSE

INNER CIRCLE GUIDELINES for LEONORIAN WITCHCRAFT
A Universal Tradition

KNOW YOURSELF
Use 'Self' control.

.

With tolerance, patience, and understanding as your tools.
Strength, heart, and wisdom as your guide.

.

Logic is The Thing That Is.
Work with the event only.
Superstition, knee-jerk reactions, and
hysterical thinking don't solve anything.
Work with the event only.

.

Take the importance off it.
Remember, it's two steps forward, one step back.

.

Know that you are the funniest thing on two legs.

.

Always imagine a little smile hovering in the middle of your forehead..

.

Now, become Nothing.

.

Self pity is poison to the human spirit.

.

Perspective is always based in Understanding the
Three Great Circles of Magic.

.

DOCTRINE and DOGMA
As taught within
THE GREAT CIRCLE OF THE ORDER OF THE RED ROSE

INNER CIRCLE GUIDELINES for LEONORIAN WITCHCRAFT
A Universal Tradition

Explore your reaction to this Question and Answer:

Teacher: "How are you?"
Reply: "Good."
Teacher: "Do you still have everything?"
Reply: "Yes."
Teacher: "Where?"
Reply: Place your hand on your lower belly and say "Here"
Teacher: "And very nice too."

·

In this context, remember, no matter what your gender:
Keep your Mind and your Legs always open
in the Service of your Craft.

·

Mind over matter starts with knowing yourself.

·

You are god. You are the devil. Yours is the choice.

·

Know that matter can neither be created nor destroyed.

·

Everything is, was, and will be - with no beginning and no end.
Everything shall be again, yet never be the same.

·

The Cycle of Creation happens Once and always.

·

DOCTRINE and DOGMA
As taught within
THE GREAT CIRCLE OF THE ORDER OF THE RED ROSE

INNER CIRCLE GUIDELINES for LEONORIAN WITCHCRAFT
A Universal Tradition

And the most important thing to consider:

We are real and not real at the same time.
We live within the 'Law of the Paradox'.

To experience, understand, and use this Law is one of the main aims and outcomes of the Study and Practise of Inner Circle Metaphysics and Leonorian Witchcraft.

Ipsissima
Leonora xx

21 DAY PREPARATION FOR INITIATION

At least once a day, every day for twenty-one consecutive days
from and including the day you agreed to Begin:

Contemplate what we have discussed over time, along with
Part One of the Initiation information described on the next page.

Be kind to yourself and don't jump into the rest of the ritual without
using the twenty-one days of preparation to review these things
and to make sure you are truly called to this Study.

You have twenty-one days, no more no less,
to decide if you wish to continue.

You may discontinue at any time within these twenty-one days.

On the twenty-first day - no sooner, no later - if you have decided and are

Certain

that you are Willing to Proceed...

You may take the Next Step

And Meet me at the Mirror.

Until then, Contemplate the following...

21 DAY PREPARATION FOR INITIATION
Part One

"Now let go of all intolerance, self pity, and vanity."

You will be required to let go of these ideals and replace them with tolerance, patience and understanding of yourself.
You will be required to do this 'at will' - on command – many times during the course of your magical practice.
No matter which path you follow.

It's called - 'self' control.

In this context self control means the ability to control your perception of reality and how you react to it.

It's also called "The Great Work".

At a higher level it's called "Mind Over Matter".

It goes hand-in-hand with "Know Thyself".

It might be the only thing you ever practise.
You may find yourself becoming adept in many other areas of magical practice and yet never master this.

Remember, this practice is not used to change others.
They have their own paths to follow.

So consider what it means to *you* to let go of these things.

How do they manifest in you?
Is it possible for you to overcome them?

See if you are comfortable with the results of your thoughts.

Consider this for the next 21 days to be sure you are Willing to Proceed.

The Initiation Ceremony is published elsewhere, for Adepts only.

MIRROR WORKINGS

MIRROR RITUAL

Create your Sacred Space by lighting three candles in front of your mirror.

Stand or sit in front of the Mirror so that you can see your face above the candles.

Look at your face, look at your eyes.

Look at that part of your forehead, just below where your Third Eye would be.

And, just slowly, look at yourself.

Look at your face.

Look at your forehead.

Listen to your silence.

And

Let

Go.

Drift and Gaze and Know that the Mirror reflects all things.

Everything you are, and Everything you are not.

Everything that is, and Everything that is not.

All That Is

and

All That Is Not

The Mirror reflects Everything.

Allow it to reflect all this as you continue to gaze at your forehead.

MIRROR RITUAL

Let the shadows and the light dance across your
face and change shape as they will.

Let the faces come and go.

Let them smile and frown as they will.

Breathe slowly and gently.

Gaze at your forehead until you can
no longer see your reflection.

As soon as you imagine, or feel, or think that your
reflection has disappeared - even if only for an instant..

Stay there for a moment, then start to come back.

Deliberately blink your eyes.

Take a deep breath through your nose and
exhale strongly through your mouth.

Shrug your shoulders.

Bow towards your reflection and all the
visitors that came to see you.

Thank them.

Extinguish the candles.

This is powerful magic!

You may use it for yourself whenever you need to
but if you wish to pass it on to others please
refer them to the whole of this text and
tell them it came from me.

With love
Leonora

MIRROR RITUAL 1
Introduction to the Inverted Pyramid

Create your Sacred Space by lighting three
candles in front of your mirror.

Stand or sit in front of the Mirror so that you
can see your face above the candles.

Look at your face, look at your eyes.

Look at that part of your forehead, just below
where your Third Eye would be.

And, just slowly, look at yourself.

Look at your face.
Look at your forehead.

Now, I'm just going to touch the top of your head.
There's a contact point at the top of your head.

Gently imagine there's the tip of a pyramid sitting there.

Just imagine.

And this pyramid stretches outwards and up – and
reaches out to the farthest part of the universe.

And it's balanced nicely right on the tip at the top of your head.

In this pyramid there's everything you wanted to be.

And you can choose to take whatever part of that you need
and allow it to flow in through the top of your head.
And the parts you don't want can flow right
back out into the pyramid, and away.

The Mirror reflects Everything.
Everything that is.
Everything that is not.
Everything you are, and Everything you are not.

Allow it to reflect all this as you continue to gaze at your forehead.

MIRROR RITUAL 1
Introduction to the Inverted Pyramid

Gaze at your forehead until you can no longer see your reflection.

Let the shadows and the light dance across
your face and change shape as they will.
Let the faces come and go.
Let them smile and frown as they will.

Listen to your silence.

And - Let - Go

Drift and Gaze and Know that the Mirror reflects all things.

All That Is.

And

All That Is Not.

As soon as you imagine, or feel, or think that your
reflection has disappeared - even if only for an instant..

Stay there for a moment, then start to come back.

Deliberately blink your eyes.

Take a deep breath through your nose and
exhale strongly through your mouth.

Shrug your shoulders.

Bow towards your reflection and the visitors that came to see you.

Thank them.

Extinguish the candles.

This is powerful magic!

You may use it for yourself whenever you need to
but if you wish to pass it on to others please
refer them to the whole of this text and
tell them it came from me.

With love
Leonora

FOUR POINTS OF THE PYRAMID

Four Points of the Pyramid Meditation

All converging at the Second Chakra point, in
the lower belly just above the pubic bone.

This meditation can be used within a Ritual context in
front of your Mirror after the Circle Opening and Raising
the Energy of the Signs, or as a stand-alone technique
for invoking strong focus and inspiration, or to assist in
healing, soothing, energy raising, or restoring Balance.

Method:
If you are performing the meditation after a Circle
Opening, your arms will already be in position,
so you can just continue from there.

Otherwise:
Sitting, or standing with feet shoulder width apart.
Invoke the First Breath and raise your arms
to the Inverted Pyramid position.

Slowly exhale, and as you lower your arms, imagine the tip
of the Inverted Pyramid also lowers from the top of your
head, and down, to settle just above the pubic bone.

Your arms are now by your side, a small distance
from your thighs, elbows slightly bent,
palms forward, thumbs outward.

Four Points of the Pyramid Meditation

Hold that image, close your eyes, and allow a second, upright
pyramid to come in from far below you towards the point
of the first one, so that the tops of each pyramid meet, and
the bases are reaching up and down away from you.

Now imagine two more pyramids coming in from each side,
their tips joining the first two, sides touching, and bases
stretching to either side, away from you into infinity.

For ease of impression, these can be visualised as Triangles,
however they are actually pyramid shaped 'funnels'.

A very bright yellow/white light starts to shine like a small
sun at the point where the tops of each pyramid meet.
At that point in your body. Your lower belly.
Your Hara. Your second Chakra area.
However you name it.

Allow the light to shine at the meeting point.
The tops of all four Pyramids.

Intense at the centre with rays
and beams extending in all directions.

Let it shine and glow, while you sit or stand
with your legs slightly apart, arms by your side,
palms extended down and facing forward, head up.

Four Points of the Pyramid Meditation

Inhale and exhale deeply three times while
allowing the Sun to shine with strength at
the points where the pyramids meet.

Keep your focus there and let your body fill with Light.

Slowly move your arms across the front of your body to
the Acolyte's LOW First Position - the fingers of the
right hand resting on the palm of the left, with the
elbows almost straight so the thumbs meet
just below the pubic bone,

Holding the Shining Sun in your arms.

Inhale and raise your arms to the Inverted Pyramid
position, open your eyes, look at your Reflection and
begin A Calling and Drawing In, or other Ritual.

Or the Grand Ceremony as written.

Or simply smile and offer Cupped Hands Thanks
to complete the meditation.

In the Service of your Craft.

Ipsissima
Leonora xx

A CALLING AND DRAWING IN

A Calling and Drawing In Ritual for Daily Use
And as a prelude or closing for other Ceremonies, Meditations and Rituals.

Light your candles and stand in Starting
position in front of an Altar Mirror.

Understanding what the Mirror represents, and what it Reflects:
Invoke the First Breath, and raise your arms
to the Inverted Pyramid position.

Gaze gently upon the centre of your forehead, and
Agree that The Mirror reflects all things.

Then State out loud to your Reflection, to
your forehead, and to the Mirror:

"I call upon YOU. I call upon YOU. I call upon YOU.
Everything you are, and everything you are not.
Everything that is, and everything that is not.
All that is, and All that is not."

Lower your arms to your side as you State:
"And I draw that Energy into me."

Return to Starting position, breathe in the First
Breath, and Raise your arms upward again.
Imagine the Insignia hovering just above your
head and State firmly THREE times:

"I wear the Crown of Strength, Heart, and Wisdom."

Then lower your arms to your side, allow the Insignia to
start drifting downwards, filling your body
and gently resting there, and say:
"And I draw it into me."

A Calling and Drawing In Ritual for Daily Use

With hands still resting by your side, fingers
towards the Earth, repeat THREE times:

"I now let go of all Intolerance, Self-pity, and Vanity."

Return to Starting position, breathe in the
First Breath, and raise your arms once more.
Slowly lower them to your side, and
State TWICE as a Matter of Truth:

"I draw in the Energies of Tolerance, Patience, and Understanding."

As your arms reach your side, palms offering
forward, fingers towards the Earth, Agree out loud:

"I am filled with the Wisdom of Tolerance,
Patience, and Understanding."

Repeat: "In the Service of the Craft." THREE times.

Allow the Energy of the Cycle of Creation to swirl
around you for one deep breath in and out.

Inhale. Exhale, and Bow towards your Reflection
as you slowly Affirm three times:

"So be it."

Offer "Cupped Hands" Thanks to the Altar
and the Ancient Covens in the Mirror.

This completes the Ritual.

Ipsissima xx

Sit Like a Witch

For use during any personal Working where you
want to feel more open, or more intimately connected
to the Energy of the Ritual you're doing.

Sit on the floor or other flat surface **with the soles of your
feet together**, and your knees as close to the floor as you can.

If you can't manage that, kneeling, or sitting cross-legged will do.

If that's not possible you can stand and lean back
against a wall, chair, or table, with hips forward.

Find your comfortable position, then gently place
the palms of your hands on the floor behind
you, so that your back is SLIGHTLY arched.

Lean backwards, gently resting your weight on the
palms of your hands, breathe in and lift your
Heart chakra/upper chest towards the sky.

Exhale, and relax into the position for as long as you like.

We're not aiming for heroics here, so no need to
push anywhere near your pain threshold.

The position is held at least as long as it takes to expand your
chest and belly, and offer your energy towards the Mirror,
the Altar, or your Teacher, and to comfortably
respond to our Question and Answer:
(explained in the Doctrine and Dogma)

Sit Like a Witch

Teacher: "How are you?"
Reply: "Good."
Teacher: "Do you still have everything?"
Reply: "Yes."
Teacher: "Where?"
Reply: Carefully lift one hand, place it on your lower belly and say "Here"
Place your hand back on the floor behind you.
Teacher: "And very nice too."

If no Teacher is present at the time, you can ask yourself the questions, and using the same movements, give your replies to the Mirror/Altar.

If doing this in a Ritual setting, Open the Circle Round and Round first, then Sit in the middle of the Circle facing the Mirror/Altar and perform the Question and Answer.

In a group, Open the Circle, then everyone Sits facing the Altar, while the Leader asks the Questions.

Then stand, thank Mirror/Altar/Teacher with Cupped Hands, or Invoke the First Breath lifting arms to the Inverted Pyramid position as usual, and Raise the Energy of the Signs.

In the Service of the Craft.

Ipsissima xx

I am Here

Strength Heart and Wisdom
A Sacred Agreement and Understanding of the Magical Condition

Initiates Version

This version of the Working should be done separately from A Calling and Drawing In and is best done at night as a stand alone Meditation for Mirror Work, in conjunction with the Sit Like Witch Ritual as follows.

Open the Circle Round and Round and Raise the Energy of the Signs.

Lower your hands to your side, palms forward.

Inhale. Exhale.

Become Nothing as suggested in Mirror Rituals 1 and 2.

Gaze at your Reflection then answer these questions slowly and with Certainty:

I am Here

Strength Heart and Wisdom
A Sacred Agreement and Understanding of the Magical Condition

Teacher: "Who are you?"
Answer: "I am Here."

Teacher: "What are you?"
Answer: "I am Here."

Teacher: "When are you?"
Answer: "I am Here."

Teacher: "Where are you?"
Answer: "I am Here."

Teacher: "Why are you?"
Answer: "I am Here."

Teacher: "How are you?"
Reply: "I am Here"
(Teacher: "Do you still have everything?"
Reply: "Yes."
Teacher: "Where?"
Reply: Carefully place your hand on your lower belly and say "Here"
Teacher: "And very nice too."
Return your hand to your side.)

Teacher: "Time and Place?"
Reply: "Nowhere, and Here."

Inhale and exhale slowly while you consider these things, then shrug your shoulders, and gently roll your head from side to side. Blink your eyes a few times, exhale firmly, and come back.
Cupped Hands Thanks closes the Ritual, as usual.
Ipsissima xx

for ACOLYTES

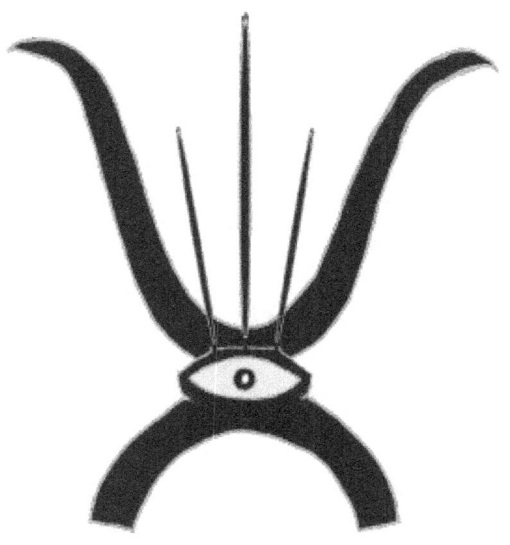

Strength Heart and Wisdom

4
DEEPER

A Calling and Drawing In Ritual
And as a prelude or closing for other Ceremonies, Meditations and Rituals.

ACOLYTES and ADEPTS VERSION

Light your candles and stand in LOW Starting
position in front of an Altar Mirror.

Invoke the First Breath, and raise your arms
to the Inverted Pyramid position.

Gaze gently upon the centre of your forehead, and
Agree that The Mirror reflects all things.

Then State out loud to your Reflection,
to your eyes, and to the Mirror:

"I call upon YOU. I call upon YOU. I call upon YOU
Everything you are, and everything you are not
Everything that is, and everything that is not
All that is, and All that is not"

Lower your arms to your side as your REFLECTION States:
"And We draw that Energy in."

Return to LOW Starting position, breathe in the
First Breath, and Raise your arms upward.

Imagine the Insignia hovering just above your head
as REFLECTION States firmly:
"We wear the Crown of Strength, Heart, and Wisdom."

Inhale, Exhale and utter TWICE:
"We are Strength, Heart, and Wisdom."

Then lower your arms to your side, allow the Insignia
to start drifting downwards, filling your body
and gently resting there, and say:
"And We draw it in."

A Calling and Drawing In Ritual

With hands still resting by your side, fingers
towards the Earth, repeat THREE times:

"We let go of Intolerance, Impatience, and Self-pity."

Return to LOW Starting position, breathe in the
First Breath, and raise your arms once more.

Slowly lower them to your side, and State
TWICE as a Matter of Truth:

"We draw in the Energies of Tolerance, Patience, and Understanding."

As your arms reach your side, palms offering forward,
fingers towards the Earth, Agree out loud:

"We are filled with the Wisdom of Tolerance,
Patience, and Understanding."

Repeat: "In the Service of the Craft." THREE times.

Allow the Energy of the Cycle of Creation to swirl
AS IT WILL for one deep breath in and out.

Inhale. Exhale, and Bow towards your Reflection
as you Affirm slowly three times:
"And so it is."

Offer "Cupped Hands" Thanks to the Altar and
the Ancient Covens in the Mirror.

This completes the Ritual.

Ipsissima xx

Circle Opening and Raising the Energy of the Signs
Leading into A Calling and Drawing In

ACOLYTES and ADEPTS VERSION

Performed as though Calling the Quarters but with Inner Circle Understanding and Intent.

Light your candles, Create your Space and Invoke
the Circle Opening Ritual as follows:

Starting at the 'top' of the Circle and facing the Altar, turn left
and walk around the circumference three times, speaking
the following lines slowly enough so that
one line takes one revolution:

1st round: "I walk the Circle round and round"

2nd round: "I walk the Circle round and round"

3rd round: "I walk the Circle round and round, and Round"

Then, looking at the Signs on your Mirror, Invoke the First
Breath, raise your arms to the Inverted Pyramid position and

Call the Energy of the Signs into the Circle.

Raising the Energy of the Signs
ACOLYTES and ADEPTS VERSION

Performed as though Calling the Quarters but with Inner Circle Understanding and Intent.

Holding the Inverted Pyramid position throughout, state out loud to each Sign in turn:

To The Horns of Fate:
"I call upon All Potential to bring Everything that Is, and Everything that Is Not into the Circle."

To the Sign of Transmission:
"I call upon Transmission to bring Information into the Circle."

To the Eye of Self Knowledge:
"I call upon the Eye of Knowledge to bring Wisdom into the Circle."

To the Sign of Change:
"I call upon Change to bring Possibility into the Circle."

To the Spirit of Water:
"I call upon the Spirit of Water to bring Desire into the Circle."

To the Bridge of Life:
"I call upon the Bridge of Life to bring the Life Force into the Circle."

To the Centre of Power:
"I call upon the Key to bring the Mysterious Knowledge of Time into the Circle."

A Calling and Drawing In
ACOLYTES and ADEPTS VERSION

Then gaze upon your Reflection, as usual, and State out loud

"And,,, I call upon YOU. I call upon YOU. I call upon YOU.
Everything you are, and everything you are not.
Everything that is, and everything that is not.
All that is, and All that is not."

Lower your arms to your side while your REFLECTION States:
"And We draw that Energy in."

Return to LOW Starting position, breathe in the First
Breath, and Raise your arms upward.

Imagine the Insignia hovering just above your head
as REFLECTION States firmly:
"We wear the Crown of Strength, Heart, and Wisdom."

Inhale, Exhale and utter TWICE:
"We are Strength, Heart, and Wisdom."

Then lower your arms to your side, allow the Insignia
to start drifting downwards, filling your body
and gently resting there, and say:
"And We draw it in."

With hands still resting by your side, fingers
towards the Earth, repeat THREE times:

"We let go of Intolerance, Impatience, and Self-pity."

A Calling and Drawing In
ACOLYTES and ADEPTS VERSION

Return to LOW Starting position, breathe in the First
Breath, and raise your arms once more.
Slowly lower them to your side, and State
TWICE as a Matter of Truth:

"We draw in the Energies of Tolerance, Patience, and Understanding."

As your arms reach your side, palms offering forward,
fingers towards the Earth, Agree out loud:

"We are filled with the Wisdom of Tolerance, Patience, and Understanding."

Repeat: "In the Service of the Craft." THREE times.

If you have cleansing, healing, or any other Work for yourself or others
PERFORM IT HERE.
If a Supplicant is present within the Circle, they must be seated facing
the Mirror, or lying on their back, head towards the Altar, arms by
their side palms up, legs straight and feet bare, and they MUST
have been present within the Circle from the beginning.

When you have completed that part of your Work, the Supplicant
remains relaxed where they are until the Ritual is finished.
(See ADDENDUM for more information)
Otherwise:
Allow the Energy of the Cycle of Creation to swirl
AS IT WILL for one deep breath in and out.

Inhale. Exhale, and Bow towards your Reflection
as you Affirm slowly three times:
"And so it is."

Offer "Cupped Hands" Thanks to the Altar
and the Ancient Covens in the Mirror.

This completes the Ritual and Closes the Circle.

ADDENDUM

ADDENDUM
FOR ACOLYTES and ADEPTS

Please note:
The Great Circle of the Order of the Red Rose is
hierarchical, as is the Practise of Leonorian Witchcraft.

This is because the outcomes of some of our more advanced Rites and Rituals require a level of expertise possibly not Understood by Neophytes, casual observers, and Friends on the Fringe.

Therefore, for group meetings, even though this Powerful Rite is led by a Middle Circle Acolyte or an Adept – particularly if there will be cleansing, balancing, or other Work done – if Neophytes or Supplicant Visitors are involved the 'general' version of Raising the Energy of the Signs and the 'daily' version of A Calling and Drawing In Ritual should be used.

Otherwise use the versions for Acolytes and Adepts.

Having said that,
This is designed to be an inclusive Ritual that can be used "Fit for Purpose" the same way as other, similar Circles work.

You can do it solo or in a Coven group - and can also bring in requests for cleansing, rebalancing or other Work from outside the group.

This can also be done one-on-one, or with the Coven present.

Of course, all that needs to be planned in advance, so that offerings, contributions, donations, or tributes have been given before the Ritual takes place.

Also, Raising the Energy of the Signs can be done while facing the Mirror, or walking anti-clockwise to each Sign where it would appear if drawn on the floor around the Circle.

Or there can be one person per Sign standing around the Circle Raising each one in turn, while the Leader remains at the Top facing inwards, towards the Circle and in front of the Altar until the last Call.

ADDENDUM

Then everyone except any Supplicants who might be there,
who remain QUIETLY in position from the beginning
to the end of the Ceremony, turns to face the
Mirror, Invokes the First Breath, and "I call upon You" …

If a member or members of the group request cleansing,
rebalancing, or other Work, they can take part in the Opening
and the Drawing In up to the final "Service of the Craft" statement.

Supplicants are then called (e.g. In the Service of the Craft... We
Call *name(s)*) and the Work commences.

In a group setting, someone other than the Leader
comes to help the Supplicant gently to their feet.

After walking with them to the Altar, the helper
takes a step back, 'bows' and walks away.

Otherwise the Leader helps them rise and walks them to the Altar.

The Supplicant remains in place until the Work is done.
Uttering "thank you" finalises the Work for them.

The Leader kindly nods an acceptance - no words are needed.
The Supplicant steps away.

Other Supplicants are then called: "We Call", as before.
If no other Supplicants are present "And so it is" is
Invoked as usual, and the Ritual is complete.

The Leader offers Cupped Hands thanks to the Altar and the Ancient
Covens in the Mirror, turns and repeats Cupped Hands
thanks with the group, and the Ritual is complete.

Solo Workings follow the same form, but the Ritual
is completed with "And so it is" and thanks.

Ipsissima xx

for INNER CIRCLE ADEPTS

Strength Heart and Wisdom

5
DEEPEST

A Hex Chant and Banishing Ritual

DISCLAIMER
This is powerful magic!

You may use it for yourself if you need to, but beware
of passing it on to others who might not have
the expertise to deal with the results.

Be sure YOU have the expertise to deal with the results.

We do not follow the Rule of Three, but Nature always exacts a price.

Knowing that Balance is invoked.

Having considered all other possibilities and options.
If you are certain and sure that the situation warrants self-defence.

This simple Chant repeated with Desire and Full Knowledge is used.

And follows this form exactly.

Focus!

When dismissing or wanting to remove a problematic
situation, or when burning or burying an item that
is causing distress, repeat this chant over
and over until the deed is done.

*

Gone for good and gone
Gone for gone and good!

*

When the deed is done, stop the chant and
immediately drop the thought.

Leave it alone.
Forget about it, and walk away.

May you never Thirst.

Ipsissima xx

Death and Passing Over Utterance
Spoken by the Coven Leader.

Light your candles, Create your Space and Invoke
the Circle Opening Ritual and Raising the Energy of the Signs.

Follow with A Calling and Drawing In Ritual.

Immediately after declaring "In the Service of the Craft" three times.

Utter:
"We send warm thoughts of Opening the Way for our cherished Friend."

Name Here

**Gathering repeats the name.

Utter:
"May their Path be one of comfort as they choose their Time.

**Gathering repeats: "May their Path be one of comfort."

Utter:
"A candle lights the Way."
Celebrant or chosen person/people walk slowly to light a candle
or candles of their choosing on or near the Altar.

When they are lit, Utter:
"We burn a candle for a Loving Wish towards
loved ones, family and friends."

**Gathering repeats "We burn a candle for a Loving Wish."

Eulogies are heard now.

Death and Passing Over Utterance

When all has been said, Utter:
"Inhale, exhale, as we take a moment's
silence in remembrance."

Allow about a minute to pass, then
cough softly to bring awareness.

Utter:
Name here was Known and will be remembered.

Farewell, dear Friend.
The stars shine forever."

**Gathering repeats "The stars shine forever."

The formal ceremony is closed by the Leader offering Cupped Hands thanks to the Altar and the Ancient Covens in the Mirror, then turning towards the gathering and affirming "And so it is" one more time as they quietly depart.

May you walk in the Darkness and the Light.
Ipsissima xx

Release and Excommunication Ritual
Spoken by the Coven Leader to the One Who is Leaving.

The One Who is Leaving must first return all Certificates,
Rituals, and documents of Membership.

With those returned items on a chair nearby
Light the candles and the incense.

Stand facing the Altar Mirror, with the One
Who is Leaving, present or not, on the
right, facing the Mirror.

Inhale.

Take a small step to your left, away from them, then move
your left foot diagonally towards the Mirror, your
shoulders angled at 45 degrees between the
Mirror and the One Who is Leaving.

Exhale.

Invoke the First Breath and lift your arms
to the Inverted Pyramid position.

Lower your arms to your side.

Understanding what the Mirror represents, and what it Reflects:
With elbows bent from the waist, palms up and forward as
though offering a Gift, state out loud to the Mirror, and
to the One Who is Leaving, whether present or not:

Release and Excommunication Ritual

"I Release you.
I Release.
I Release you.
I Release.

I Release you from your Obligation,
or your Promise, or your Vow.
As it was before you joined us
(pause and inhale)

(on exhale)
So it is Again.

(inhale – on exhale firmly state)
NOW."

Take their Certificate(s), their Insignia, and their
Third Order Chiefs' welcome.
Put them together, tear them in half and
immediately place them back on the chair.
Then State Clearly and with Certainty.

"It's Done.
Farewell"

The One Released then moves away quickly and silently.

Turn to face the Altar.

Thank the Ancient Covens in the Mirror with a small bow forward.
(Don't use Cupped Hands thanks here).

Extinguish the Candles.

The torn documents are immediately either burned,
buried, or simply put in the rubbish bin.

This completes the Ritual
Ipsissima x

TRANSFORM

Circle Opening and Raising the Energy of the Signs
A Transformational Mind Over Matter Version for personal use.

**Performed as though Calling the Quarters but with
Inner Circle Understanding and Intent.**

Light your candles, Create your Space and Invoke the
Circle Opening Ritual as follows:

Starting at the 'top' of the Circle and facing the Altar,
turn left and walk around the circumference three times,
speaking the following lines slowly enough
so that one line takes one revolution:

1st round: "I walk the Circle round and round"

2nd round: "I walk the Circle round and round"

3rd round: "I walk the Circle round and round, and Round"

Then, looking at the Signs on your Mirror, Invoke the First
Breath, raise your arms to the Inverted Pyramid position and

Call the Energy of the Signs into the Circle.

Circle Opening and Raising the Energy of the Signs
A Transformational Mind Over Matter Version for personal use.

Holding the Inverted Pyramid position throughout,
state out loud to each Sign in turn:.

To The Horns of Fate:
"I call upon All Potential to bring Everything that Is,
and Everything that Is Not into the Circle and into my life."

To the Sign of Transmission:
"I call upon Transmission to bring
Information into the Circle and into my life."

To the Eye of Self Knowledge:
"I call upon the Eye of Knowledge to
bring Wisdom into the Circle and into my life."

To the Sign of Change:
"I call upon Change to bring
Possibility into the Circle and into my life."

To the Spirit of Water:
"I call upon the Spirit of Water to
bring Desire into the Circle and into my life."

To the Bridge of Life:
"I call upon the Bridge of Life to bring
the Life Force into the Circle and into my life."

To the Centre of Power:
"I call upon the Key to bring the Mysterious Knowledge
of Time into the Circle and into my life."

Then perform the Adepts version of A Calling and Drawing In.
Closing that Ritual completes the Work.

Ipsissima xx

I am Here

Strength Heart and Wisdom
A Sacred Agreement and Understanding of the Magical Condition

Acolytes and Adepts Version

This powerful version of the Working is meant for Adepts
and those Second Level, Middle Circle Acolytes
who are well versed in Paradox Law.

Although also a stand-alone Meditation, it's best done
at night as a Magical call to extend the Liminal
and begin Ritual or Mirror Work.

Open the Circle Round and Round and
Raise the Energy of the Signs.

Lower your hands to your side, palms forward.

Inhale. Exhale.

Become Nothing as suggested in Mirror Rituals 1 and 2.

Gaze at your Reflection then answer these
questions slowly and with Certainty:

I am Here

Strength Heart and Wisdom
A Sacred Agreement and Understanding of the Magical Condition

Teacher: "Who are you?"
Answer: "Here."

Teacher: "What are you?"
Answer: "Here."

Teacher: "When are you?"
Answer: "Here."

Teacher: "Where are you?"
Answer: "Here."

Teacher: "Why are you?"
Answer: "Here."

Teacher: "How are you?"
Reply: "Here"
Teacher: "Do you still have everything?"
Reply: "Yes."
Teacher: "Where?"
Reply: Carefully place your hand on your lower belly and say "Here"
Return your hand to your side.

Teacher: "Time and Place?"
Reply: "I am Nothing, and I am Here."

Inhale and exhale slowly between
worlds, and continue on to your chosen Ritual.
Otherwise, shrug your shoulders, gently roll your head from
side to side, blink your eyes a few times, exhale firmly, and come back.
Cupped Hands thanks closes the Ritual, as usual.
Ipsissima xx

Flow Between Worlds

In the Service of the Craft
For Acolytes and Adepts

Similar in method to Raising the Energy of the Signs, this powerful Working is a stand-alone technique used to strengthen communication with the Known and the Unknown, and deepen even further your experience of the Liminal.

It can also be used to enrich the Grand Ceremony or the Adepts version of A Calling and Drawing In.

Take Heed.
The Transformational SOLO version
replaces 'Us' with 'Me'.
Be Ready.

For the Grand Ceremony, or A Calling and Drawing In, enact this Working after uttering "In the Service of the Craft" as written.

As a stand-alone technique, Open the Circle,
Raise the Energy of the Signs, then..

Invoke the First Breath and raise your arms
to the Inverted Pyramid Position.

With your eyes resting gently on your Reflection throughout...

Flow Between Worlds

In the Service of the Craft
For Acolytes and Adepts

Think about the First Sign and Declare:
"Everything that is, and Everything that is not Flows to us and from us"

To the Sign of Transmission: "Information Flows to us and from us."

To the Eye of Self Knowledge: "Wisdom Flows to us and from us."

To the Sign of Change: "Possibility Flows to us and from us."

To the Spirit of Water: "Desire Flows to us and from us."

To the Bridge of Life: "The Life Force Flows to us and from us."

To the Centre of Power - the Key: "The Mysterious Knowledge of the Past, Present, and Future Flows to us and from us."

Perform the Working once during A Calling and Drawing In (then "And So It Is"), and before the second Four Points of the Pyramid meditation during the Grand Ceremony.

Perform the stand-alone Working three times, whether in a group or solo.

After the third time through, Utter "In the Service of the Craft" three times. Lower your arms to your side and Agree "And So It Is" three times. Inhale. Exhale strongly and gently shrug your shoulders.

Offer Cupped Hands Thanks to the Altar
and the Ancient Covens in the Mirror.
The Deed is Done.

In the Service of the Craft.
Ipsissima xx

TRANSCEND

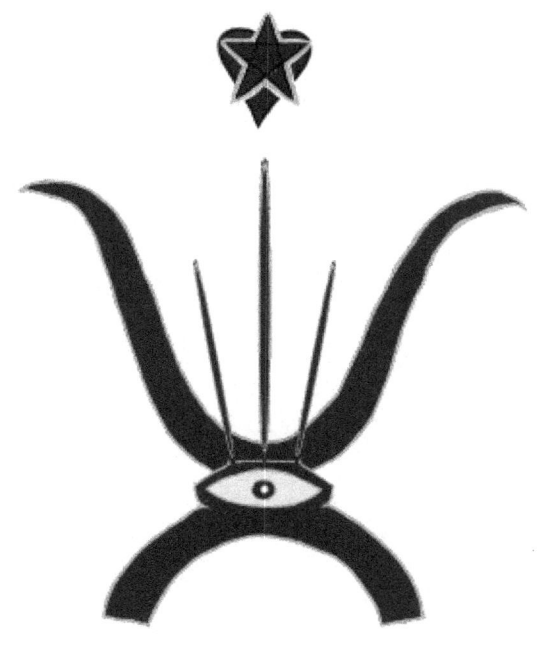

In the Service of the Craft

6
THE GRAND CEREMONY

The Path of the Grand Ceremony

The Grand Ceremony follows a Path that guides the Practitioner
towards a powerful, experiential Understanding of the Cycle
of Creation, the Life Force, and the Law of the Paradox.

And Opens the Mind to a full and complete
Liminal Merging with The Other.

Be WARNED!

It is a pure and thorough Experience.
Make sure you are Ready.

First the Space is prepared.

Then the First Acknowledgment of the Form takes place:
Observing the Crown and Chalice Insignia.

We then Draw awareness towards the physical generative
area, and agree the Life Force manifests there in every
individual, regardless of gender:
Sit Like a Witch.

Followed by the first Immersion into the Liminal
using the 'As Welcome' version:
I Am Here.

The Practitioner is now Between Worlds and
ready to Create a sacred place:
Open the Circle Round and Round.

The Path of the Grand Ceremony

Experience of the Liminal is strengthened using
the Four Points of the Pyramid meditation.

Followed by the First Invocation to The Other:
Raising the Energy of the Signs.

Now a deep Experiential of the Gateway to Awareness is Invoked:
Allow the Cycle of Creation to envelop you.

Once and Always.

The Practitioner, now deeply Between Worlds and within
the Heart of the Inner Circle, enters strongly Focused
into a Sacred Blending with The Other:
A Calling and Drawing In.

Fully Liminal the Practitioner is Nowhere and Here.

Open and Free within this Sacred Space, the Practitioner
senses the Experience and nutures its Flow within
Heart and Mind, Above and Below:
Flow Between Worlds.

The Four Points of the Pyramid meditation.
When Light has filled the Body, we return by Observing the
Crown and Chalice Insignia and what it represents.

The Agreement "And So It Is" is Stated firmly three times.

Cupped Hands Thanks closes the Ceremony.

In the Service of the Craft.

Ipsissima xxi

The Grand Ceremony
For Group or Solitary work
In a Group setting the Coven Leader or an Adept calls the Rituals.

Setup your Altar and Ritual Space.
Light the incense and candles.
If preferred, start your background music.
Dim or turn off the lights.

Stand (skyclad) in front of your Mirror.
Invoke the First Breath and raise your arms
to the Inverted Pyramid position.

Look at the Crown and Chalice and acknowledge out loud:
"Tolerance brings Strength
Patience brings Heart
Understanding brings Wisdom".

If solitary, consider this quietly.
In a group, the Leader states out loud:
"The Crown of Strength, Heart, and Wisdom is also
The Chalice of Tolerance, Patience, and Understanding.
One, States of Being within our Order - the other, the Tools of our Craft.
We draw one in, and immerse ourselves in the other.
They are not the same, but they each contain
their - alternate - attributes - equally."

Lower your arms to your side and perform
a standing version of Sit Like A Witch.

Perform the 'As Welcome' version of I Am Here.

Open the Circle Round and Round.

Perform the Four Points of the Pyramid Meditation,
either as called by the Leader, or in your own Time if Solo.

The Grand Ceremony

When the Light has filled your body:
Invoke the First Breath and raise your arms
to the Inverted Pyramid position.

Raise the Energy of the Signs.

Lower your arms as you allow the
Cycle of Creation to envelop you.

Once and Always.

Perform the version of A Calling and Drawing In that
is right for you, through to a single, whispered
"In the Service of the Craft".
Invoke the First Breath and raise your arms
to the Inverted Pyramid position.
Flow Between Worlds.

Stand quietly and forever Between Worlds for one full Breath.
Perform the Four Points of the Pyramid Meditation.

When the Light has filled your body:
Invoke the First Breath and raise your arms
to the Inverted Pyramid position.

Observe the Crown and Chalice and State out loud:

"Strength equals Tolerance
Heart equals Patience
Wisdom equals Understanding".

Lower your arms.
Repeat "And So It Is" three times.

Cupped Hands Thanks closes the Ceremony.
In the Service of the Craft.

Ipsissima xxi

7
DISCOVER

The Three Great Circles of Magic

Diagram of the Levels Within the Three Great Circles of Magic

Diagram of the Levels within the Three Great Circles of Magic

---

Outer Circle First Level: The Use of Worship and Faith
This is the most popular Magic Practice in the World.

Outer Circle First Level

The Use of Worship and Faith
This is the most popular Magical Practice in the World.

This includes all Religions and Philosophies that use Prayer or Supplication to any kind of Deity, and those who refute the existence of any kind of Deity.

Outer Circle Second Level: Know Thyself while using Worship and Faith

---

This is the beginning of the Path of the Seeker. Until the decision to step beyond Faith and Worship is made, no inquiry beyond the Dogma of the chosen Faith is required. Once this step is made the Practitioner begins the journey towards greater Understanding.

Diagram of the Levels within the Three Great Circles of Magic

---
Middle Circle First Level: Know Thyself without using Worship or Faith
---

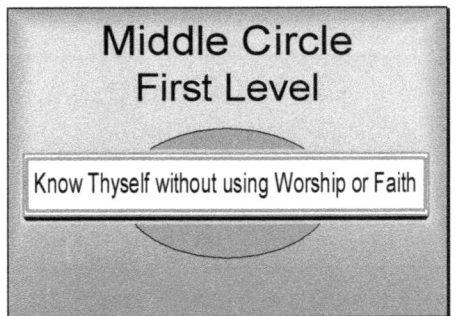

This is the place where the first understanding of Creation, and How it Occurs begins. It's also the beginning of "Occult" knowledge, because information that was "hidden" by the smoke-screen of Worship and Faith starts to be revealed here. It is the first entry of Neophytes through the Portal into the place where the informed decision and agreement to Open Your Mind is made.

From now on everything is consciously part of the Practice.

Middle Circle Second Level: Application of Logic and Self-Control
Openly exploring the Laws of Nature. Learning to "Step outside" yourself.

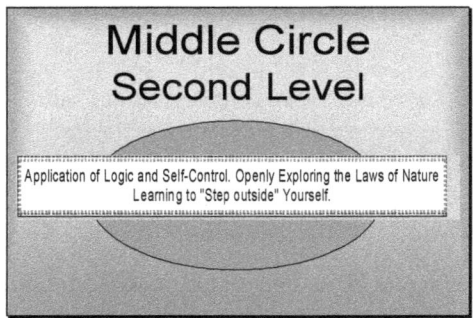

This is where the bulk of the Practice takes place. It is the Level of the Acolyte. All events, as mentioned in the description of the Three Great Circles of Magic in *"Powerful Magic – Secrets from the Inner Circle"* are studied in depth here. Includes esoteric and scientific methods. The nature of Time is introduced.

Most practitioners spend their lives working at this Level.

Diagram of the Levels within the Three Great Circles of Magic

---
Middle Circle Third Level: Continued Exploration in "split" Observations of Yourself
Introduction to the Law of the Paradox. Learning to Teach.

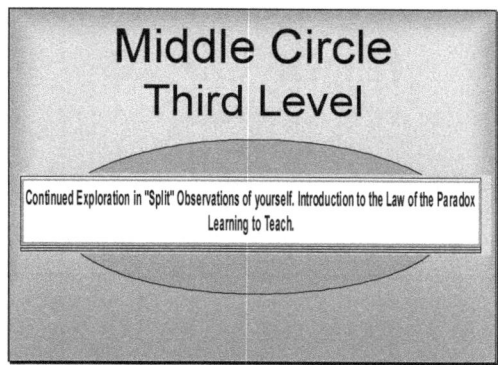

This is where the Cycle of Creation and How it Occurs is Realised, and testing for Self-control and Balance of Mind occurs. The Law of the Paradox becomes apparent to the Practitioner here, and the ability to "Step Outside" Yourself becomes second nature.

Still an Acolyte, here the Practitioner enters the beginning of their training for Mastery – often called "The Dark Night of the Soul" – and is usually unaware of the specific entry point. This is also where the ability to assist others along the Path is studied, with guidance from the Instructor. After a series of trials, tests and examinations by the Instructor, the Acolyte becomes a "Master", with a full and well-understood Knowledge of Time, Themselves, and whatever area of expertise they've chosen as the Tools for their Exploration.

Somewhere within this Level, many Practitioners will exit the Portal and Cross the Abyss back to "normal" life.

Some will Find the Inner Circle.

Diagram of the Levels within the Three Great Circles of Magic

---
Inner Circle: Full Recognition of the Law of the Paradox
Understanding Creation, and How it Occurs.

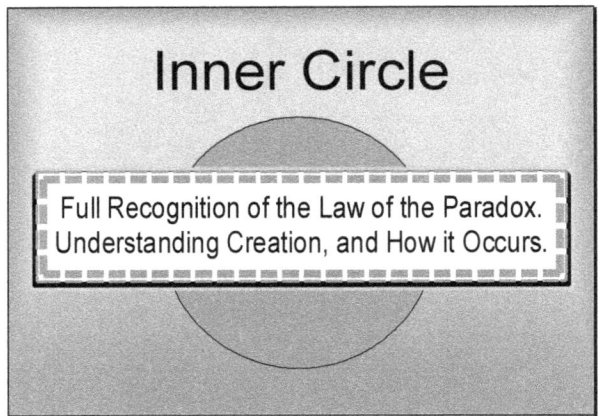

This Circle carries an implied Fourth Level relative to the three Levels of the Middle Circle, and an overall Seventh Level relative to the Three Great Circles of Magic, and itself.

This is where an Understanding of Dimensional Overview, and the Cycle of Creation becomes apparent and Usable.

The Law of the Paradox is accepted, resolved and Understood as Logical and inherent Knowledge.

The Practitioner – now an Ascended Master, or Adept – continues the Practice as a way of life, and chooses if and when to offer Information to Seekers.

It is due to the perspective gained along the Path, which culminates within the Inner Circle, that the Outer Circle method of Worship is Understood as a Magical Practice.

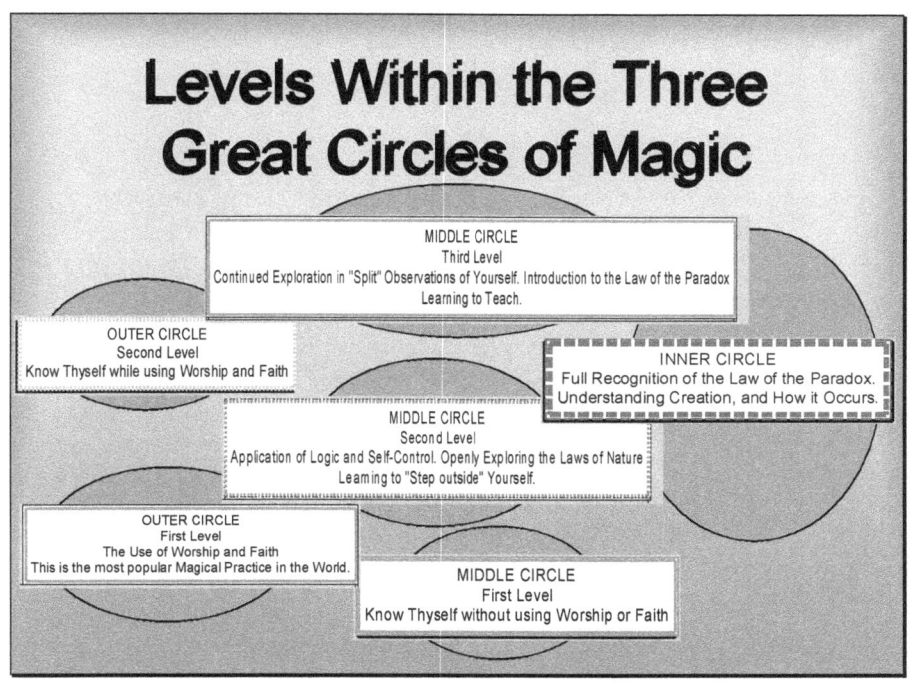

Strength Heart and Wisdom

Magic is all around us

It's time

Remove superstition from mystery

Open your mind

In the Service of the Craft

www.ingramcontent.com/pod-product-compliance
Lightning Source LLC
Chambersburg PA
CBHW031153160426
43193CB00008B/349